NEW ENGLAND INSTITUTE
OF TECHNOLOGY
LEARNING RESOURCES CENTER

SUCCESSFUL PROBLEM SOLVING

NEW ENGLAND INSTITUTE
OF TECHNOLOGY
LEARNING RESOURCES CENTER

NEW ENGLAND INSTITUTE
OF TECHNOLOGY
LEARNING RESOURCES CENTER

SUCCESSFUL PROBLEM SOLVING

A PRACTICAL GUIDE FOR THE STUDENT AND PROFESSIONAL

Maridell Fryar
Robert E. Lee High School
Midland, Texas

David Thomas
Auburn University
Auburn, Alabama

NATIONAL TEXTBOOK COMPANY • Skokie, IL 60077 U.S.A.

1983 Printing

Copyright © 1979 by National Textbook Co.,
8259 Niles Center Rd., Skokie, Ill. 60077
All rights reserved. No part of this book
may be reproduced, stored in a retrieval system, or
transmitted in any form or by any means, electronic,
mechanical, photocopying, recording or otherwise,
without the prior permission of National Textbook Company.
Manufactured in the United States of America.
  234567890ML 98765432

Preface

Successful Problem Solving is the third volume in a series of practical guides for students and professionals. While this series is designed to provide students with the tools necessary to building rewarding and satisfying careers, many of the skills presented have applications outside the business community. Each volume in this series isolates a skill basic to success in pursuing and maintaining personal and professional effectiveness.

Successful Problem Solving examines problems, goals, and obstacles; explores some common causes of unsuccessful solutions; and describes the steps in problem solving from definition of the problem to implementation of the solution. Activities and exercises, including role-playing situations, provide a realistic opportunity to apply and practice the concepts presented.

Each concise volume in the series is well organized and clearly written to ensure maximum learning in or outside the classroom. Each is a brief introductory guide to mastering the techniques essential to basic skills that must be utilized in managing our lives. Whether these guides are employed as supplements or incorporated within a year curriculum, they provide valuable advantages to those who will be entering today's highly competitive and complex world.

Contents

Introduction — 1

I. Problems Examined:
   The Need for Problem Solving — 4
   Definitions — 4
     What is a Problem? — 5
     What is a Goal? — 6
     What is an Obstacle? — 7
   Choice: The Essence of Problem Solving — 8
   Common Causes of Unsuccessful Approaches to Problems — 9
   Personal Factors Related to Problem Solving — 10
     Age — 10
     Sex — 11
   Some Ways Individuals Make Ineffective Choices — 12
     Ignore Problems — 12
     Make Hasty Choices — 12
     Behave Dogmatically — 12
   Some Ways Groups Make Ineffective Choices — 13
   Summary — 16

II. **Problems Solved:**
   The Steps in Problem Solving 17
   The Problem Solving Attitude 17
     Helpful Attitudes for Individual Problem Solvers 17
       Focus on What is Ahead 17
       Look at a Particular Problem 18
       Be Goal Related but be Realistic 18
       Put Yourself in the Solution 19
     Helpful Interpersonal Attitudes for Group Problem Solvers 19
       Avoid Interpersonal Conflicts 19
       Promote Variety 19
       Put Aside Prior Commitments 20
   The Problem Solving Sequence 20
     Define and Limit the Problem 22
     Analyze the Problem and Gather Data 24
     Establish the Criteria for Possible Solutions 26
     Suggest all Possible Solutions 29
     Select the Best Possible Solution or Solutions 31
     Plan for Implementing the Solution 33
     Summary 35

III. **Problems Practiced:**
   Discussion and Role Playing for Problem Solving 37
   Brain Teasers for Warm-up 37
   Exercises for Understanding Personal Factors in Problem Solving 39
   Exercises in Defining and Limiting the Problem 41
   Exercises in Analyzing the Problem and Gathering Data 43
   Exercises in Establishing Criteria for Possible Solutions 46
   Exercises in Suggesting All Possible Solutions 49
   Exercise in Applying the Six Steps in Problem Solving 49

Introduction

Successful Problem Solving has been written as an integral part of a series of books that is geared to important life skills. Problems exist for every person, and successful solutions for those problems can determine our personal happiness, job satisfaction, and sometimes even our very existence. Because this is true, we hope that this book will prove helpful to each person who uses it.

We believe that it will certainly be usable in a wide variety of classroom and business settings. In fact, as we wrote, we kept in mind the following audiences as potential readers of this book:
1. *High School:* Classes in basic speech, in vocational and work study programs, and in technical and career English.
2. *Community Colleges:* Classes in the vocational and work study area, in adult continuing education programs, and in courses preparing students for the G.E.D.
3. *Business and Industry:* Short term training sessions and workshops for executives, supervisors, and other employees which are aimed at giving assistance in coping with problems which are work related.

We have both long been interested in and tried to use problem solving ourselves in both personal and professional situations. While in the process of writing this book, one of us had an experience that illustrated again the value of knowing and using a systematic approach to solving problems. Although the experience had its humorous overtones, it also had the potential of being frustrating, inconvenient, and embarrassing for a number of people.

In the late spring, one of the authors was scheduled to travel with three other adult sponsors and five students to the capital city of her state in order that the students could compete in the State Tournament. Students and sponsors from all over the state would converge on the city for that weekend. When plans were being made, motel reservations were very difficult to get, and so were highly prized. On the appropriate date, after putting in a full day at school, the group loaded school vehicles and prepared to leave. One sponsor, realizing they would arrive very late, called the motel to reconfirm their reservations and to ask that the rooms be held late for them.

Following a seven hour drive, the group arrived at the motel. The sponsors went inside to the desk, announced the name of their school, and waited for room numbers and keys. The lobby was filled with other groups of young people and adult sponsors. All noise ceased as the new arrivals and everyone else in the lobby waited for the room clerk's response. The young lady behind the desk appeared very close to tears as she fumbled with a group of cards and then turned to the author to announce, "I don't have any reservation for your group."

In total disbelief, the author responded, "But we called you for confirmation before we left our school!"

The young lady took another careless look at the cards in her hands, took a deep breath and repeated, "I don't have reservations for you!"

The other sponsors standing in the lobby began gathering students and leaving, satisfied that the story they had gotten was the same one being given to others. Some went to phones to try to find other lodging, and others simply went to their cars. Once more, the author, with a stridency in her voice, repeated, "Look again! I know you have reservations for us!!"

The tears in the desk clerk's eyes were no longer a hint; they were a reality. Her voice shook as she said, "I have no rooms." Fighting anger and frustration, the sponsors conferred. One went to try unsuccessfully to secure other accommodations, one went to report to the waiting students, and the author turned back to the desk. Before the author could say anything, the young lady said, defensively and tearfully, "It's not my fault! I have a headache, and I can't help you at all."

"Young lady," replied the author with some asperity, "We are not talking about who is to blame and crying won't solve this. If it would, I'd cry, too!

These students are tired. It's late, and they have to compete in the morning at 8:00. Are you sure there are no beds for us?"

The young lady answered, "I told you, I don't have any rooms."

Suddenly the author realized that the problem had not been adequately defined. "No," she hastily answered, "I asked if there were *beds* available."

The desk clerk's face lit up, and she exclaimed, "Of course! We have two parlor rooms. They have couches in them that fold out into beds." Then her face fell again, "But, they don't have a bathroom."

The author probed again: "But is there a bathroom in the motel which is not being used?"

Again, the young lady replied, "Well . . . the sales office has a full bath and shower."

"Fine!" the author announced hastily. "We will take them for the night. We will worry about tomorrow night, tomorrow!"

There is no intention of having you believe that the ideal accommodations in a motel are sleeping on a hide-a-bed in a parlor room on the fourth floor, and commuting to a bathroom adjoining the main lobby. That, however, seemed much preferable to solutions some groups found that night in the very overcrowded city. The real point is that rational problem solving, even under stress, is possible.

It is our sincere expectation that after carefully studying and practicing the skills explained in this book, you will have the ability to approach problems in a systematic way. There is, however, no money back guarantee. There is only a strong assurance from personal experience that it can work.

I. Problems Examined: The Need for Problem Solving

What This Book Is About

Jerry's biology grade falls, and his parents talk about making him quit the track team if he can't raise it. Carla and Eduardo need some additional income to try to buy their own home. Mrs. Hayes feels trapped at home now that her children are grown, but she can't locate a job she likes.

Groups face problems, too. A sporting goods company sees that it will make 100 percent profit this year. This looks like a nice problem to most of us, but the owners realize this means higher taxes unless something is done with the extra money. Should they expand the store? Should they invest in stocks and bonds, or donate to charity or local causes? Which of these ideas might work out to be the best solution?

Consider another example of a group problem. One of the most common problems faced by our cities is the decay of downtown areas. Groups like the Downtown Merchants' Council must work out ways to combat their problems. They must discuss their mutual parking and traffic woes and find ways to compete with the suburban mall's acres of free parking. Unless this problem is solved, some downtown stores will be forced to close their doors, and thus weaken the rest.

Have you noticed that some people and some groups are better at solving their problems than others? Do you ever feel that your problems are too much to handle? Have you ever wanted to throw up your hands in surrender? Or, have you ever made a decision that turned out to be wrong, without knowing the reason you went wrong? As we look at these questions, you'll see that you are not alone. We all have problems, all through life, in all that we try to do; the big difference is in how we try to solve them. Some methods of problem solving are better than others.

You can control many of your problems if you know how. And you can learn how! This means that you can choose to be successful in solving your problems or you can choose to fail. If you can't solve your problems because you don't know how, and you don't try to learn the best approach, your failure is the result of your choice not to succeed.

This book is about how you can succeed when you work to solve your problems. You can't escape your normal share of problems. You must learn to confront them. Not only must you face them, but you must solve them. Some people know the best way to find good answers to their personal, financial, romantic, academic, and job problems. You, too, can learn how to solve your problems in the best way—a way that works.

What Is A Problem?

A problem is what you have when an obstacle stands in the way of a goal you want to reach. When we begin to write this book, we looked at many books and articles on successful problem solving. All our sources agree on what is meant by a problem. Whenever a barrier or obstacle stands in the way of reaching your goal, you have a problem. If you have no goal, then by definition you can have no problem. Or, if you have a goal, but nothing prevents you from reaching it, again you have no problem. Only when you are frustrated in trying to reach your goal is there something you must solve.

Problems can be divided into individual and group problems. Any time more than one person (such as a group) faces a problem, it gets more complicated. You have the problem itself, and you also have extra problems caused by the difficulties people have in working together. Although the basic problem solving system is the same for both individuals and groups, it helps to consider them separately. In Part II of this book, we explain how problem solving can be done by both individuals and groups—successfully.

What Is A Goal?

A goal is that which you want to achieve. The goal of a football team is to win the championship. This means it must win all or most its games. The goal of a business is to make money. The goal of a nation is to grow stronger and to be secure in a changing world. The goal of a student is to graduate; or it may be to learn a trade or a skill. Your goal in reading this book is to learn to make life easier by handling your problems better.

The famous psychologist, Abraham Maslow, shed some light on the meaning of goals. He studied man's basic needs and pointed out how we're led to act to fulfill them. According to Maslow, there are five basic needs which can be thought of as our most primary goals.

1. *Life.* Your most basic need is life itself. You must survive in order to begin to think about any other goals. You meet this primary need by using food, water, a house to live in, etc. If you lack any of the things you need to live, nothing else matters until you get it.

2. *Safety.* Once you've met the need of survival, you next most important goal is to be safe from harm. You avoid danger and threats of danger at almost any cost. You meet this need by watching over your children, putting locks on the doors, and obeying traffic signals. Fear moves people to act almost as much as life itself moves you to act.

3. *Love.* After you have life and safety, you want to love and be loved by someone else. You fulfill this need first in your family; then, through courtship, marriage, and starting your own family. When you feel unloved, you act to correct the situation. You might even leave an unloving situation at home and seek to establish a new one.

4. *Esteem.* Beyond sharing love with someone else, you want to feel wanted, liked, and respected by all your friends. This goal is related to life in a larger group, the community in which you live. As with love, you seek out niches in life where you can earn the esteem of others.

5. *Self-Actualization.* Finally, you have your own unique personal needs and goals, after your basic needs are assured. You want to be able to express yourself, to use your talents to create things, and to enjoy life. Of all the basic goals, achieving selfhood is the one you can never fulfill perfectly. You can quench your thirst for water, but you always feel a thirst for self-actualization.

An important point must be mentioned about these five goals or needs. They come in a certain order, that is, they form a hierarchy. Only when one of the goals is fulfilled do you move up to the next one. Fortunately, in our richly blessed nation, nearly all of us can meet these basic goals. You can get things you need for survival, security, love, and esteem. You can even make progress towards reaching your own goals of self-actualization. In more primitive countries, people might not reach their highest goals. Some people's lives are so deprived that they can't reach the level of esteem in their community. Merely living, guarding against threats, and having a family turn into major struggles. Most of us are not so severely deprived. We should feel good that we can strive with more success towards our basic goals.

This hierarchy applies to groups as well as to individuals. Take a business, for example. Company officers must first make sure the business *survives* in the market place. They must plan for all the angles to make sure all *threats* to its corporate life are overcome. Every business is also concerned with its *status* in its field. Once a business is thriving, you can be sure it will be interested in *innovating creativity* and *achieving excellence.*

You can probably think of other groups which are motivated by Maslow's hierarchy. Committees, clubs, and other groups are also concerned with their survival, safety, esteem, and selfhood. In short, all human entities, whether individuals or groups, have goals to reach.

It gets harder when you have more than one goal at the same time. If you have multiple goals, you might spread yourself too thin. Groups might also fall into the trap of trying to reach more than one goal at a time. Members may assume everyone shares their personal goals, when the truth is that some members have exactly opposite goals. When this happens, problem solving becomes an impossible task. That is why it's so important for groups to agree on a clearly understood goal from the outset. Without it, successful problem solving is difficult if not totally out of the picture.

What Is An Obstacle?

We have been talking about one term in our definition of a problem, a goal. Now let's look at another term, an obstacle. Remember, a problem is what you have when an obstacle stands in the way of achieving your goal.

An obstacle is that which stands in your way. Let's make an analogy between problem solving and a car journey. Think of your destination as your goal. You want to drive from your home to the beach for a vacation. You start out in the car; and if there are no obstacles, you'll reach the beach and have your vacation on schedule.

On the way, however, you might have a flat tire. Then you would have a problem. Or, you might come up to a detour in the road. The Highway Department is building a new bridge, and they have barricaded the road. Or, halfway to the beach, you remember you left the oven one, and you have to go back home to turn it off. These are examples of how something can stand in your way in reaching your destination. In these cases, the obstacles can be overcome. Your vacation will be delayed only as long as it takes to overcome each obstacle.

Most problems are like that. As long as you have a clear goal in mind and ample resources to reach it, solving problems is just a matter of adjusting to the obstacles that come up. Part II explains a tested, step-by-step method that works to help you solve your problems successfully.

Choice: The Essence Of Problem Solving

In this book we want to look at problems where you must make a choice. Wherever your choice can influence your success or failure, you should know the best ways to go about choosing. We won't say much about types of problems where you have no choices to make.

For instance, a puzzle is a problem with only one right answer. All you have to do is fit the pieces together, and the picture emerges. A problem in arithmetic has only one correct answer. "Farmer Brown has a square pasture that is 40 rods on each side. How many square rods are there in the pasture?" This is a problem, but its solution is simply a matter of knowing how to multiply 40 × 40. Our book is not about single-choice tasks such as puzzles and arithmetic tests.

Another type of problem this book cannot help you with is the kind in which your decisions are made for you. There are many situations where you are required to follow someone else's decisions. Choices are made, but not by you. You might work for a company where the boss makes all the decisions, and you're hired solely to carry out orders. Or, you might be a youth in a home where your parents dictate, "As long as you are under our roof, young lady, you'll come in by midnight on week nights!" At some point, your parents decided that a midnight curfew was the solution to a problem. The only part you are permitted to have is to live with it. These situations only require you to search for the answer, or to learn the rule that applies. You are not expected to make a hard decision.

When we rule out single-choice puzzles and choice-free situations, that still leaves many areas where this book can help you and the groups you join. A young man in high school has a few hundred dollars saved up from doing yard work. A friend offers to sell him a used motorcycle for $250. Should he buy it or not? A young woman makes it through high school. The very next summer she meets a nice young man whom she likes a great deal. Should she go away to college? A Sunday School class begins to lose attendance. The teacher is a wonderful person, but his lessons are dry and dull. What should be done?

income is limited in many cases. The husband, meanwhile, is in a new job where he wants to prove himself and become qualified for promotion. The young woman works hard to be a good homemaker, wife, and person in her own right. She often feels a conflict within herself over trying to meet all these goals.

Problems often arise when these strong needs of the husband and wife collide. At the time when the husband feels he must work long hours on the job, his wife wants him to devote increased attention to their home situation. She wants him to help her and appreciate her for all that she is doing. Sometimes, she wants him to sit down and listen to her when he is tried or tense over his job, when what he wants from her most of all is a calm, quiet home environment. They each want more support and understanding from the other. This couple's needs and desires are very different from those of teenagers, from whose ranks they so recently emerged.

3. *Midlife.* In their thirties and forties, a married couple sometimes develops new problems. The husband might have reached a plateau or dead end on his job, which causes him to be frustrated. The wife might feel that life has passed her by now that the children have grown to an age where her motherly care is not needed. Both men and women must make major readjustments in their lives in order to be happy.

These differences between people at different ages are relevant to problem solving. You have different goals at different times in your life. Not only that, but different obstacles crop up to frustrate the fulfillment of your goals. Most importantly, different approaches to the solutions of your problems are suggested. Within a common age group, these distinctions may be less pronounced since a common perspective is shared. When a problem solving group consists of people whose ages span a wide range, it may be much harder for you to reach common understandings because you see things from different points of view.

Sex

Another important factor in how people cope with their problems is sex. By this we mean that males and females approach the process of problem solving in different ways. Let's make it clear that we aren't making judgments about these sex-based differences. Rather, we are merely reporting what research has generally found to be true. You can think of many individual exceptions to the remarks we made about age differences. Likewise, there are many exceptions to these points about sex differences. Although these observations about men and women will usually be true, we must recognize that times are changing. What is true of society today may not be true tomorrow. Changes are being brought about by forces such as the women's movement.

Psychologists and others have written extensively about sex differences in group communication in their professional journals. Here are some of the findings related to how men and women differ in solving problems in a group.

1. *Interaction Patterns.* When men and women work together in a group, men tend to take the lead and women tend to follow. Men talk more, and interrupt women more than women interrupt men. When men say something to the group, they are more likely to talk about the problem under consideration, whereas women are more likely to express their emotions. Women frequently express agreement with what men initiate, and they are generally more cooperative and sympathetic to others.

2. *Task Performance.* In general, men are more oriented towards solving tasks, whereas females are more interested in communication and personal problems that arise within the group itself. In terms of solutions, men are bolder and innovative; women are more conservative. Women conform more closely to the norms when it comes to accepting major changes which are suggested.

3. *Leadership.* Men are more agressive, assertive, and self-confident than women. Men make more suggestions, and defend their ideas with more force than women. Women depend on men and tend to be more passive. When women try to be leaders, they are less sure of themselves. They are more likely to yield to objections made by men.

These sex role differences mean that, in general, men are more efficient at group problem solving than women. This is especially true when a problem solving group includes both sexes.

How do women get their way in such an environment? Two female researchers addressed this important issue. Paula B. Jackson and Jacqueline D. Goodchilds told us their findings in a recent issue of *Psychology Today* magazine. They wrote, "Generally women learn to get their way by helplessness rather than by anger or expertise." They went on to explain that in their study of 250 UCLA students, half of the women used emotional tactics such as sulking, pouting, and crying to get their way. One-fourth of the men used emotions as a tactic, but the emotion they used was anger, not passive helplessness. More men than women used logic, reason, and information to persuade others.

We must point out that this article doesn't advocate that women should use such tactics. In fact, the result gained by these tactics may be the opposite of what was intended by the women who used them. They might get their way *once,* but afterwards the group regards them as incompetent.

Why do women act that way in their efforts to solve problems? Why aren't women more confident and assertive? Another research report by Patricia S. Faunce, a psychologist at the University of Wisconsin, explains some of the reasons. In our society, women are socialized to be subordinate to men. As children, females and males are taught these patterns both directly and indirectly. Parents give a girl dolls to play with, and they protect her from rough games. Parents direct boys into team sports where hard competition is rewarded. Also, as adults, women are torn between two conflicting definitions of success. On one hand, women are expected to become trained and educated for responsibilities, yet they are measured against standards of femininity and attractiveness (to men) which run against the grain of assertive leadership in a man's world. Forced to choose the type of role they should perform, most women prefer to be feminine and attractive, not "bitchy" and aggressive. They avoid doing the things that are thought of as masculine.

But times are changing. Thanks to the persistent efforts of many people, sex roles that penalize women who try to be successful problem solvers are declining. Schools and churches are starting to lead the way in teaching women how to be more assertive and logical when faced with problems. Women are doing so without becoming unduly aggressive or losing their femininity. Men are beginning to like women who know how to use effective problem solving techniques. "Lady bosses," formerly unpopular with men and women alike, are becoming more widely accepted in business. These developments can help to solve the problems of women. In turn, more effective women can work with groups better to solve common problems.

Some Ways Individuals Make Ineffective Choices

1. *You Ignore the Problem.* Sometimes you are willing to put up with problems which could be solved if you tried. You might think that life is supposed to be hard. You might think that the obstacles in the way of achieving your goals are placed there as a punishment for your sins. You might feel too weak or unintelligent to be able to do anything about your problems.

Ignoring a problem never solves it. In fact, to repress problems always causes stress. Stress has many bad effects. It can interfere with your effectiveness in all areas generally; and it can cause health problems such as ulcers and heart attacks. As a rule, ignoring a problem is a very poor choice to make.

2. *You Are Too Hasty.* There's a saying in the Navy, "Do something, even if it's wrong!" This is the other side of the coin we talked about above. Sometimes it may be better to do something than to do nothing, but to do something wrong isn't a good solution, either. Your problem will remain, not because you ignore it, but because you choose a poor solution. In fact, doing the wrong thing usually causes new problems to deal with along with the original one.

3. *You Are Too Dogmatic.* You might be aware of what your problem is, and you might be able to see more than one way to solve it. However, your chance

of making the wrong choice is magnified if you aren't truly open-minded about your options. Advance commitment to your first choice is the same as a hasty decision. What good does it do to know about alternatives if you don't consider them?

Some Ways That Groups Make Ineffective Choices

Studies have been made of how a group works when it has a task, but no training in problem solving. Invariably, the group fails to solve its problem. The group does come to some sort of agreement, but it's apt to be for the wrong choice. The reasons for this stem from the group becoming emotionally involved without giving logical thought to the problem solving process.

An ineffective group goes through four phases. In the first phase, called *orientation,* the group is polite and friendly as it tries to become acquainted. Every member wants to be cooperative in solving the task together.

Second, in the *confrontation* phase, someone pops up with an idea for how to solve the problem. The group immediately begins to discuss the suggestion, with no thought or discussion given to the problem itself. Members of an untrained group will assume they know all they need to know about it. Without exploring the problem, the group can have only a fuzzy idea about it. As a result, the group focuses attention on just one possible answer.

How does the group proceed in the second phase of discussing the proposed solution? When someone makes a suggestion, the group breaks down into two factions: those who like the idea, and those who are not in favor of it. Often, the split is related to personalities. Who does the group like most? The person who made the suggestion, or the person who objected to it?

The group can't think logically about any solution to the problem at this point since no real effort has been made to define the problem. Therefore, how can the group have a clear grasp of whether a solution is workable? At this level of conflict over whether the proposed solution is a good one, arguments become personal. Discussion centers on the qualities of the person who proposed it. There are suggestions of blame, or possibly insult, rather than logical analysis.

The third phase of the typical untrained group is the *compromise* phase. When the tension between the conflicting sub-groups becomes too unpleasant, someone offers a compromise to try to bring them all back together. Often, the compromise consists of some kind of vague generality to which both sides can readily agree without affecting any of their arguments. Notice at this point, the original problem itself still hasn't been truly discussed. The conflict over the only proposed solution is now covered up.

Finally, the group goes through the fourth phase, called *reinforcement*. They are happy to have found a compromise with which everyone can agree. Now, they rehash all the reasons they feel they should agree with it, in the form of repetition of most of the points previously made. This phase has been called "beating a dead horse." However, it is necessary in order to firm up the consensus which the group has reached. Without reinforcement, some members will fall away from the final compromise. At the conclusion of this final phase, the group feels it has covered a lot of ground. Their group feeling has been reinforced. They have made new friends and survived a conflict. They are confident they have "dealt with the problem," and "reached a solution." In reality, they haven't solved the main problem, only covered it up.

Personal emotional needs and drives can interfere with a group and lead to group malfunctions. First, some members want to use the group as a platform for the exercise of power. They lose sight of the primary mission of the group, which is to solve the problem. In extreme cases, such a member takes a "rule or ruin" attitude. In the end, the decision of the group is merely this member's decision which has been railroaded through. Second, at the other end of the spectrum, there are some group members who don't participate actively in the discussion. They withdraw, and say little or nothing at all. Either of these practices is detrimental to the problem solving process. The group should not allow an egomaniacal person or a clique of a few members to take over. On the other hand, quiet members should be drawn into the process and encouraged to express their thoughts and ideas.

Either trying to rule the group, or totally withdrawing from the group are extreme actions. There are other unproductive ways you could act towards others in a group which ought to be mentioned. People have a tendency to react to others on a personal level. You may be able to concentrate on a problem in a factual, objective manner when you are acting as an individual; but when you join other people in looking at the problem, emotional reactions arise. When your basic concern becomes the protection of your self-image instead of solving the group's task, these personal responses are called *ego-defensive*. They can interfere with the process of group problem solving.

Some of the more common ego-defenses are these: *Projecting* is believing others have your own thoughts and feelings. If you say, "He doesn't know what he's talking about," but the point is really about something you don't know, you are projecting your personal lack to the other person. *Rationalizing* is convincing yourself that some trumped-up reason exists for your actions or feelings when there aren't any good reasons. This is sometimes called the "sour grapes" reaction. Aesop's *Fables* tells the story of the fox who wore himself out trying to leap up for a bunch of grapes high over his head. He finally gave up and walked off, saying, "Oh, well, they were probably sour anyway!" *Identifying* is taking on the ideas and feelings of others just because you want to be like them. *Scapegoating* is finding a person to blame for your failures when that person isn't responsible.

These and other ego-defensive mechanisms aren't unusual. Everyone tends to react to others in the group on a personal level. What you must be aware of are the dangers of raising ego-defensive acts to a higher level of importance than the task of problem solving. Ego-defense never solves the problem, and it can get in the way of a group's success.

The common fault in all of these group malfunctions is this: *emotion replaces thought.* People lose sight of the problem and become obsessed by their emotions. The facts about the problem and its possible solutions become less important than liking other members, or being liked. The key to solving a problem successfully always comes back to using logical thought.

Summary

In this chapter, we've discussed the importance of problem solving. We have defined a problem as what you have when an obstacle stands in the way of achieving your goal. We have examined the nature of goals and obstacles. We have seen that the essence of problem solving is choice, which is a personal decision. Yet your choices are influenced by factors such as your age and sex. As a result, you are prone to make inappropriate choices in your efforts to solve your problems, such as ignoring a problem or deciding on a solution too hastily or too dogmatically. Groups, too, are guilty of covering up problems rather than solving them because it's so easy to replace logical thought with emotion.

The heart of our method of problem solving, as we'll explain in Part II, is clear thinking. There is a systematic approach to problem solving which uses intelligent choice instead of emotion. Individuals and groups alike can learn to use the method. To understand that a better way to deal with problems exists, and not to learn that method, is to choose to be a failure. To learn to analyze your problems by identifying your goals, spotting the barriers, looking at the options, and choosing the best one, is the smart way to solve problems. That is the way that works. It's your way to successful problem solving.

II. Problems Solved: Steps in Problem Solving

The Problem Solving Attitude

Problems are common to all. They demand some kind of response. How you respond, however, makes all the difference in the outcome. The very nature of problems is to create feelings of doubt and frustration. Your nature is to react with fear and emotion.

Many attitudes which you can have toward your problems can be destructive. We have looked at those attitudes and have shown you how they get in the way of solving problems. However, there are also attitudes which you can develop which are productive.

Helpful Attitudes for Individual Problem Solvers

1. *Focus on what is ahead.* When a problem presents itself, you might spend a great deal of unproductive time trying to "wish it away" or regretting actions which you believe produced it. You try to blame someone or focus on the conditions under which the problem developed. Seeing only the negative aspects

of the problem will not produce solutions. This attitude only makes the problem seem impossible.

The attitude which will produce results for you is the one which might best be illustrated by extending the old axiom, "Don't cry over spilt milk!" Go beyond that to focus on the question, "How can I clean it up?" and "How can I keep it from happening again?" These questions will lead to solutions.

2. *Look at a particular problem.* You might be often tempted to generalize your problems to the extent that they seem too big to deal with. When you do this, you are overwhelmed by the impossibility of what you must do. Instead of thinking in generalities, think in specifics. Deal with problems of manageable size. If, in truth, your problem is a big one, start with a small enough part that you can manage. Work your way through that portion and then begin on another aspect of it.

When you look at a specific problem, it helps you to consider only the facts and details which truly relate to that problem. You will not be sidetracked nor spend valuable time on irrelevant matters. When you focus on a particular problem, then you will find particular solutions which will seem more manageable.

3. *Be goal related, but be realistic.* Too often you might reject good solutions to problems because you have been unrealistic about setting goals. Certainly we would all like to live in a Utopia, but literature as well as experience tell us that such a goal is out of reach. Continuing to want a Utopia creates problems where none exist.

For example, as teachers we would like classes in which students learned for the sheer joy of acquiring knowledge. We would delight in students who cared nothing about grades but who sought to satisfy their own desire for excellence. However, since we lack classes filled with such ideal students, should we quit teaching in frustration over "bad" students? We think not. Instead, we are oriented to realistic goals. We know that grades can sometimes lead to self-motivated students. We know that students can value learning for its own sake even though they attend class for other reasons. We set a goal of offering to every student in our classes, an opportunity for learning. That goal we can deal with. It is realistic.

Goal setting is essential to good problem solving. You must not only be able to describe where you are. You must also describe where you want to be. The attitude in which you set those goals will determine how successful you will be. If your goal is reaching for a perfect situation, you may find yourself magnifying problems which you have, and ignoring solutions which could be useful.

4. *Put yourself in the solution in an active capacity.* A good attitude toward solving problems is one that begins with questions such as: "What can *I* do?";

"Where am *I* in relation to where I want to be?"; "How long do *I* have to reach my goals?" It is easy to design solutions for someone else. That, however, may not be constructive. The solution to your problem must be within your reach. This is not to say that good solutions cannot involve others. But if your solution must begin with statements such as: "If mother will . . .", or "If the student council will . . .", you have removed yourself from an active role. You have opted out of the solution to your own problem.

Helpful Interpersonal Attitudes for Group Problem Solvers

There are attitudes which can help with individual problem solving. There are also some others which are important when groups are trying to work toward solutions. In order for the group to function constructively, there are many interpersonal skills which members need to exercise. Some of them are things which are true for you any time you are in communication with others. Good listening habits, consideration of others, and sincerity must all be part of your behavior in a group. Some other specific attitudes are important to groups when they try to solve problems.

1. *Avoid interpersonal conflicts.* It is not necessary for everyone in a group to love one another in other for that group to function effectively. Otherwise, state legislatures, most clubs, and many school faculties would never be able to function. It is necessary, though, for everyone in that group to respect the opinions and rights of everyone else. When a group is involved in problem solving, many special barriers can get in the way. These cause interpersonal conflicts. A few of those barriers are special interests, defensiveness, prior commitment to a solution, and power plays by members. If you want your group to be effective, try to help avoid these. If you want to be an effective part of the group, help prevent these conditions from developing within the group.

2. *Promote variety.* A big problem with many groups is tradition. This is especially true of groups which are operating within established organizations or institutions. We have seen many good solutions for student organizations flounder on the schoals of assertions such as: "We never have done it that way!" or "The administration won't allow that!" If a group is to be effective in problem solving, it must reach for variety. It is rare that a group considers problems which are new to the human experience. Young people may not like to hear adults say so, but it is true that both groups face many of the same problems. Since these problems have been around a long time, new solutions which have not been tried may be the answer. Certainly the "system" may stand in your

way. However, you should not put it up as an obstacle before you at least try new solutions.

3. *Put aside prior commitments.* If you are to be successful as a group in solving problems, you must come together without any advance obligations to a particular solution. A great deal of research has been done in this area. All of it shows that the less time individual members of the group have to think about the problem before they meet, the more successful they are in finding solutions as a group. What occurs when members of the group have their minds made up ahead of time is obvious. They won't all agree. If they did, there would be no problem to begin with. Therefore, they each become an evangelist for a particular position. The group discussion becomes a battleground. A war erupts which has no winners. In the real world of problems, however, it is difficult to call a group together to solve a problem without their knowing something about it. Therefore, you must develop within that group a willingness to set aside previous ideas. The group task must occur before members make up their minds.

The attitudes which foster successful problem solving, whether individually or in groups, have to be learned and practiced. They are actually contrary to human nature, but they are necessary. With them we can exercise our capacity for solving problems rather than being defeated by them.

The Problem Solving Sequence

Many approaches have been outlined for problem solving. Almost every one has as its source John Dewey's book entitled, *How We Think.* In it he attempted to describe, not prescribe, how a person's thought process functions when confronted with a problem. What he discovered in his research and later described in his book was a pattern for rational thought. It is just such a pattern that we will deal with here.

We will present the problem solving sequence in six steps:

1. Define and limit the problem.
2. Analyze the problem and gather data.
3. Establish criteria for possible solutions.
4. Suggest all possible solutions.
5. Select the best possible solution.
6. Plan for implementing the solution.

Although these steps are in a sequence, they do not always follow one another in neat order. In actual practice, for example, you may get a very strong

Problems Solved   21

notion about a possible solution as soon as you begin thinking about the problem. You might stumble across some important data while you are trying to limit the problem. You might be listing a group of possible solutions and suddenly realize that you have overlooked a prime cause of the problem. However, if you know the sequence, then you can mentally file these away until the appropriate time. They will then enter the problem solving in a rational way. Otherwise, you might be tempted to believe that you had finished when you had only just begun.

By the same token, in one situation you may have to devote more time to one of the steps than you do to another. There is no set amount or proportion of time that should be allocated to the steps. It may be that you will accomplish,

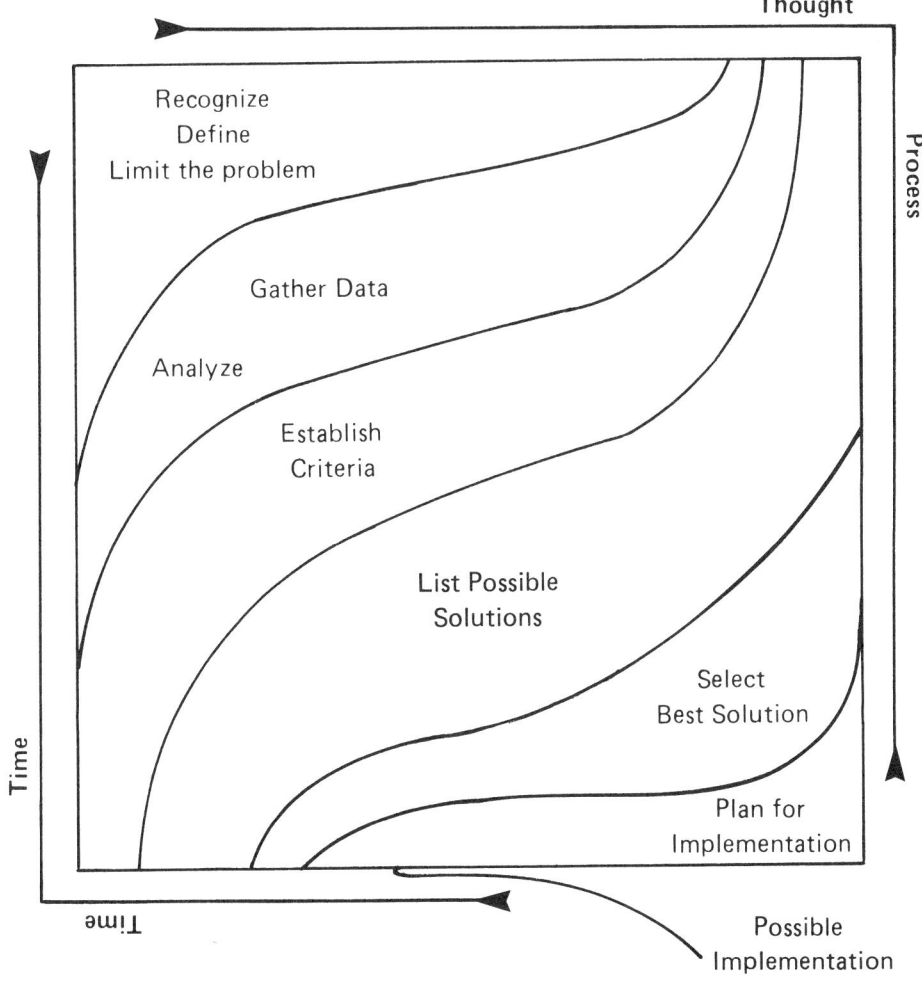

individually, a particular step quicker than a group could. On the other hand, a group might be able to overlap and work through two steps at one time. The important thing is none of the steps should be overlooked unless there is a very good reason for doing so. There is a strong interdependence between these steps. Each one contributes in some way to the other.

The diagram on the opposite page may help you visualize the way the thought process works and the time needed for each step to blend with the other. It represents the idea that, at any one moment, several steps can be taking place whether in the group, or in the individual problem solver.

Training yourself in such a rational problem solving technique will serve you well both as an individual, and when you are part of a group. It will foster the development of good problem solving attitudes. It will function with increasing efficiency as you focus on those attitudes. We will discuss briefly each of the steps in the problem solving sequence. Following each step, we will illustrate its application for an individual and for a group. It will then be up to you to become skillful in using these steps.

Step One: Define and Limit the Problem

You are always aware when a problem exists. You know this because you *feel* it. You suffer from doubts or frustrations. Knowing that a problem exists, however, does not equip you to solve it. You must do more than just feel a problem in order to solve it. The problem must be tangible. You must be able to put it into language which explains, describes, and defines it. You must be able to limit it before you can deal with it.

When you begin to define the problem, you must always state your goal first. Remember how we defined a problem. You have a problem when some obstacle stands in the way of achieving a goal. It is helpful to think of a problem as the gap between where you are and where you want to be. To state where you want to be is to state your goal. Until you can do that, you can't be sure how extensive your problem is. Also, you can never be sure you have actually solved your problem, no matter what measures you take, if you never state what your goal is to begin with.

One important skill that is part of defining and limiting the problem is the actual wording of the problem. Most problem-solving groups find it is easier to continue the steps in the process with a question. The difference between "Something is wrong with our school" and "What can the teachers do to improve our class tardies?" should be obvious. One is a statement of general feeling. The other is a question which, when fully answered, will furnish a solution to an important problem.

A question also leads very logically to the next step in the process. To say,

"Something is wrong with our school," is a dead end. It does not help you move to the next step. The question, "What can the teachers do to improve our class tardies?" immediately leads to the questions, "How bad are they now," "What is causing them," "Is there more than one group of students who are guilty?" These are questions which contribute to analysis and which lead to all the other steps in problem solving.

Limiting the problem is particularly important because it makes the problem manageable and gives focus to your decisions. You cannot, individually, or as a group, solve all the problems of the world. You cannot create the ideal situation. You must, therefore, limit the problem to those things which you or the group can deal with. This, in turn, depends on setting a realistic goal at the outset.

As an Individual: Janice, a high school senior, is increasingly uneasy and vaguely frustrated as the school year draws to a close. She finds herself irritable and unable to concentrate on her classes. She assumes that she has a case of "senioritis," and that it will pass when she finally graduates. However, the level of frustration becomes intolerable. Janice begins to examine herself in order to discover what her problem really is. She eventually acknowledges to herself that she is dissatisfied with the plans that she has made for college. At this stage, Janice has defined the problem. However, only when she admits that she is not sure that she even wants to go to college, does she limit the problem. Only by limiting it can she deal with the real problem.

As a Group: Some English teachers at Jefferson High School are disturbed about discipline in schools. They feel that students are not responsive to rules. They feel that there is not as much discipline as there used to be. They talk about it in the faculty lounge. They discuss it in the English office. Their attitudes grow increasingly negative. So far, all they have done is to "feel" there is a problem.

Dr. Miller, the principal, calls a meeting of some teachers from each department and asks them to discuss campus problems. He wants them to recommend changes in the school's policies. At the first meeting, the teachers from the English Department ask that the first area of discussion be the problem of "school discipline." Others in the group tell the English teachers that they must define and limit the problem.

First, they decide to talk only about the discipline on the Jefferson High School campus. They decide to concentrate only on discipline problems on the general campus rather than in individual classrooms. They justify this limitation on the basis that discipline with a certain classroom is a matter of individual teacher control, not overall school policy. They further decide to limit their consideration to behavior during passing time between classes and during the time immediately before and after school.

In their effort to define and limit the problem, it becomes clear that they will need to gather specific data about where problems in "school discipline" actually exist. Only after they have defined and limited the problem are they ready to continue the problem solving process.

Step Two: Analyze the Problem and Gather Data

Problem solving is a future focused activity. However, in order to design a solution successfully, you must explore the cause of the problem. This will require a look at the past. When dealing with personal problems, you will probably find it very difficult to isolate the cause. First of all, accurately identifying the cause of a personal problem may mean you must accept part of the blame. Most of us prefer to protect ourselves. It may also mean accepting the fact that there is no single cause, but rather a combination of many. To do this may mean that you cannot blame someone you want to! Identifying the cause of a problem is not to allow you to fix blame nor determine guilt. It is to equip you to design a solution which corrects that cause. It is much better to cure a problem than to treat its symptoms!

Identifying the cause of the problem is only the beginning of the analysis necessary for effective problem solving. You will also have to know what effect the problem is having and how extensive or harmful that effect is. If you campaign for a policy to correct a problem without first determining if it is a problem for anyone else, then you have been guilty of poor analysis. Furthermore, you will probably not find very much support for the solution you advocate.

When you find out how many others are affected by the problem, you will know whether or not you need to enlist the aid of groups in solving that problem. This important step also shows you whether or not information which might help you is available from other sources. It is necessary to gather the information you need in order to analyze the problem. In addition, much of the data you find will also help you formulate possible solutions. You may feel that if you have a lot of experience in a particular area then you do not need to seek more information. You should remember, however, that the things you know by experience are all seen from just your point of view. When a problem arises which needs solving, other people's ideas can be a great help. They can give you a new angle and furnish a different feel for the problem. They may agree with you. They also may show you a mistake you are making. The important thing is that you seek the knowledge of others. A college professor of the authors' often remarked that it "should not be necessary for every generation to rediscover the wheel." Neither is it necessary to proceed in ignorance in problem solving if others have preceded you. Therefore, be sure to investigate carefully so that you can take advantage of other's experiences.

All the information which you can find on the general problem area and on the particular problem you are trying to solve should be used. You will need to read widely the experience of others. You will need to seek facts, opinions, statistics, and accounts of studies in the area. A good approach to gathering data is to use the following three questions: (1) What information do I need? (2) Where could this kind of information be found? (3) How can I test the reliability of the data?

As an Individual: Sixteen year-old Stephen Tidwell has his driver's license. He has begun to ask for the use of the family car as often as possible. His mother, an active career woman, begins to feel restricted and "put upon" by his frequent requests. But she is also unwilling to purchase an additional car in order to relieve the crunch at home. Several stormy sessions increase tension in the home, not only between the boy and his mother, but also between the two parents.

Finally, the frustration is unbearable, and Mrs. Tidwell confronts her problem in order to look for solutions. She first defines the problem as one of "too many drivers and too few cars." However, that is too limited, and she revises that to "unsatisfactory distribution of cars among drivers." As she thinks about the statement, she realizes that it is her own sense of independence that she is fighting for. She also realizes that Stephen is fighting for the same thing. One cause of the problem is a valued characteristic in both her and her son.

She then spends time on the phone talking to parents of her son's friends. In an effort to explore causes and effects of a personal problem, she discovers that many others share the same problem. She also discovers that others are looking for solutions. At this point, she is ready to benefit from her research and analysis. She can now move toward solving the problem. If she had not taken the time to analyze the problem, she would have continued to be upset and to feel fuilty about a condition which she found to be common in other modern families.

As a Group: A large southwestern city is ordered by the courts to desegregate its schools. The immediate response by the community is very negative. Groups of parents storm the school board meeting and demand that the board resist the court's ruling. This solution, of course, is not legally possible. The school board is deeply concerned about two problems. First they have to design a plan for desegregation which will not penalize any ethnic group. They must also design some way to win the support of the parents and the community. Without such support, the spirit of negativism will spread to the students. Any plan would then probably fail because of student attitudes.

The board defines the causes of the parental resistance as a fear for their children. The parents are also reacting to media coverage of other desegregation plans. They are angry at federal intervention in their local schools. Most of all, they fear the unknown. The board goes immediately to community leaders. It sends representatives to other cities which have had a record of successful and peaceful integration. It sets up parent groups to start work on the design of a desegregation plan. All of these groups operate as sub-groups of the school board. The board does group research into the cause and extent of the problem. As a result of that research, they are able to solve problems by either eliminating their cause or by neutralizing the effects. The data gathered gives clear indications of needs. The use of that data isolates possible solutions.

Step Three: Establish the Criteria for Possible Solutions

At this point in the problem solving sequence, you will first begin to concentrate on possible solutions. If the first two steps have not been properly done, you will find yourself in difficulty here. An absolute understanding of the nature, extent, and cause of the problem is necessary before setting about to design a solution.

Assuming that you have done the first two steps, you must now begin to apply very specific questions to the problem in terms of the solution. Questions such as "Where do I want to be in the future?" and "What conditions must exist before this problem is solved?" It is important here to remember that you are not thinking in terms yet of *what* you will do. You are thinking in terms of what has to be true of *anything* you do. You have to decide ahead of time, for example, if money is going to be a factor in your choice of solutions. You might select an entirely different pair of shoes if "money is no object" than you would if you have already determined that the cost can not exceed $15.00. If you are confronted with a problem in your marriage, you must decide ahead of time what solutions you will consider. For instance, divorce may be out of the question because of religious beliefs. When you set criteria which the solution must meet, then you are setting up guidelines by which you will later choose among many solutions. Unless you set the criteria before the solutions are explored, you may waste time on solutions you could never use. You may overlook some which you could use.

One thing that must be considered in setting criteria for solutions is the "area of freedom" or the power of either the individual or the group. If you attempt to solve problems and have not included the legal or natural limits of your group in the criteria for solution, you will produce confusion and frustration. For example, the student council of the high school may recommend changes in student dress codes, but it does not have the authority to implement the change. A group of labor negotiators may have the ability to ask for more fringe benefits, but it does not have the power to grant them. The limits of the individual or the group must be included in the criteria.

After you have decided on the criteria which you will use for selecting solutions, you should rank them in order of importance. If one criterion is *absolute,* then any solution would have to meet it. On the other hand, if they are all options you can decide on, you need to know beforehand which you see as the most important.

Remember, too, that the statement of criteria should be very specific. If you use words such as "efficient," "good," "helpful," etc. you will not have clear ideas of what you want to accomplish. Criteria should be worded as questions to be answered by the solution or as clear and specific statements of conditions which the solution must meet. For example, a statement criteria might be: "Must not cost over $500 for entertainment. Must be entertaining and amusing to the members and their families." An example of questions to be posed might be: "How convenient is the location to the members? How large is the room? How many people can be seated at once?"

At this stage of establishing criteria, you should remember your total life goals. The one problem you are attempting to solve exists within a framework of your whole life. There may be things within that broader framework which will dictate some of the criteria that any solution must meet. Consider for example that you face a problem at work. Can you change jobs? Can you move to another location? Do you have time to retrain? Money, time, and location are just a few of the standard considerations which may be reflected in the criteria you establish.

As an Individual: Mr. Sanchez is the sponsor of the Student Council at Crocket High School. He is disturbed by the lack of attendance at the council meetings. He carefully analyzes the causes of the problem and collects data about its extent and effect. He concludes that attendance is low because the council meets before school at 7:30 a.m. Students would rather sleep. He now must determine certain criteria which any solution should fulfill.

Mr. Sanchez decides that any solution should change the time to a better one. He decides that any change should continue to put the responsibility for attendance on the student. He also determines that the new time should be long enough for the meetings, but should not penalize those with after-school jobs. Finally, he decides that the change of time should still allow the council to use the Study Hall room for its meetings.

Setting up these criteria before he actually considers alternative times for council meetings allows him to evaluate each new time against a checklist. He can eliminate quickly those suggestions which do not fit the criteria.

28 *Successful Problem Solving*

As a Group: In the period immediately after World War II, the Air Research and Development Command gave one of its research groups a task. It was to develop a dehydrated survival ration that would keep a man alive for 10 days under conditions of active Arctic survival. This group had been trained in the scientific problem solving sequence. They first made a list of what they would demand to be true of whatever ration they developed. They came up with six criteria:
1. The ration must be reasonably pleasant to taste.
2. It must not make the survivor thirsty.
3. It must make the survivor feel full.
4. It must have at least the minimum required calories.
5. It must be capable of being packaged.
6. It must be capable of being stored for long periods without ruining.

Once the research group had established these criteria, the direction of their research was also established. Each new attempt was measured against the six criteria. Since the group had agreed that all six must be met, failure to meet one meant rejection of the product.

As a Group: Several years ago, scientists in a large company developed a new mouthwash. They assured the company that it was the most effective mouthwash ever developed. Laboratory tests indicated that it was highly effective against common bacteria in the mouth which produce bad breath. However, every effort of the company in marketing the new mouthwash was met with only limited success. The money loss began to be appreciable. The company president finally gave orders that a solution had to be found, or the product was to be removed from the market.

Officers of the company conducted surveys in order to isolate the cause of the poor sales. They discovered that the product did not taste like other mouthwashes, which were generally sweet. They found that the public was not ready for a mouthwash that did not taste good. They agreed that two criteria must be met by any solution which was found: (1) it must improve sales, and (2) it must not decrease the effectiveness of the product.

Researchers immediately went to work attempting to change or to disguise the taste. Changing the formula, however, diminished the effectiveness of the mouthwash. Therefore, these attempts were rejected because they did not meet one of the criteria.

An ad agency was then employed. It looked at other products which also had obvious flaws but which were successful in the market. It determined that there was a principle at work which could be stated, "accentuate the negative—turn a minus into a plus." They devised an advertising campaign which was based on the claim, "It may not taste good, but it works." They emphasized "a clean, sharp taste," "sweet and gooey mouthwashes are just a cover-up," "cure the cause of bad breath," and other slogans which left a sense of a medical approach to the problem of bad breath. Sales escalated. The establishment of specific criteria determined the direction of the solution.

Step Four: Suggest All Possible Solutions

The term "brainstorm" is usually applied to this step. This term suggests a picture of a storm of thought which produces a torrent of ideas. This is probably an accurate description of this step. At this stage in problem solving, whether you are working individually or in a group, you have clearly defined the problem, analyzed it, and set up certain criteria which a solution must meet.

You should now begin to list all the possible solutions to the problem. Anything goes. Your suggestions should be aimed at the specific causes of the problem which you have uncovered. However, it is also possible for a solution to offset the effects of the problem. For instance, if you are sick, the doctor will probably prescribe medicine to kill the virus that makes you sick. This is an attack on the cause of the problem. For some ailments, it may be more effective to prescribe medicine than to relieve the symptoms. Most allergies, for example, can't be cured. Medicine can be taken to furnish relief from the worst symptoms of sneezing and breathing problems. This is an attack on the effects rather than the cause. Either way, you end up by feeling well again. What is important in this step in problem solving is that you sit down and make a list of every possible solution you can think of for the problem. Every idea should be recorded as it occurs. A flow of ideas is urgent.

In fact, there are four cardinal rules for brainstorming: (1) No criticism until the process is finished. (2) The wilder the ideas, the better. (3) The more ideas, the better. (4) Combine and improve as you go. One thing you must do in problem solving is to keep an open mind, to allow room for all possibilities to be considered. The only way to insure this is to list all possible solutions before any judgment is made.

The concrete nature of an actual pen and paper list is helpful during this stage. It allows you to spend several different sessions on brainstorming without losing the results between times. It gives you a specific reference point when it is time to evaluate and select solutions. It also preserves for future reference those suggestions you reject. Most of all, it requires specific description in language of ideas which might be too abstract to deal with otherwise.

One approach to this step might be to use what has been called "directed thinking." That is, devise a list of questions or categories by which to check your solutions. You can then use the checklist to remind yourself of some you may have omitted. Some suggested questions are:

1. *Have I considered all the barriers?* Have I found a way to remove the barriers, to circumvent them, to make them ineffective?

2. *Have I considered my own goals?* Could I revise goals if the barriers seem insurmountable? Can I delay goals if time is a factor?

3. *Can I adapt what I know?* What else is like this? What other ideas does this suggest? Does anything in the past seem similar?

4. *Can I change what I have?* Could a change of color, sound, form, shape, or motion make a difference? Are other changes possible?

5. *Can I add to things?* Can I add to what I already have? Would more time, greater frequency, more strength, more money solve things?

6. *Should I lessen things?* Can I take away some elements? Can I make something shorter, smaller, lighter? Can I divide something?

7. *Can I substitute?* Can I substitute people, elements, places, materials, processes? Can I substitute my approach?

8. *Can I rearrange what I have?* Can I put things in a different order? Can I put my actions in a different sequence?

9. *Can I combine things?* Can I blend things, combine actions, ideas or goals in some way?

There are many other questions which might remind you of possible solutions. Explore your own mind and try to exhaust every possibility. The longer the list of possible solutions, the greater the probability that you will have one or more which will be satisfactory and effective.

As an Individual: Eleven year-old Jennifer has sold greeting cards. She has worked hard and has had a successful venture. When all the orders are filled and the company has been paid, Jennifer has $43.00. Her next concern is how to spend the money. Her parents suggest that she put it in the bank. Her older brother offers to go "halves" on some record albums they both like. Jennifer talks first about new clothes, then about using the money for entertainment, and then again about saving it. Her indecision begins to be irritating to the family.

Jennifer's dad brings her a pencil and a pad of paper. He says, "Jennifer, let's play the problem solving game. You have $43.00. I want you to write down all the things that money could buy which you would like to have." Jennifer works at length and finally presents a long list to her dad. He then directs her to put an estimate beside each one of how much money it requires. Next, he asks her to rank them in the order of which she wants most.

As Jennifer begins to work through the long list, she comments to her mother, "Putting everything down on paper makes some of the things look silly and some look impossible." Her comment is a fair summary of how important this step can be to the individual's problem solving process.

As a Group: Jon and Sue Kim feel a real need to cut back on their family expenses. They take the record of family spending for the last four months and discover that they are spending 40 percent of their total income on food. They believe they have found the cause of their financial problems. They decide that whatever solution they find, it must not endanger the family's health by reducing nutrition.

They then ask their children to share in a brainstorming session with them by listing all the possible ways the family might cut down on food costs. During a ten-minute session in which everyone contributes suggestions, the following items are listed:

1. Give up desserts.
2. Experiment with eggs, dried peas, soy beans, and cheese for meat substitutes.
3. Persuade everyone to diet or fast one day a week.
4. Sponge off the neighbors at least once a week.
5. Join a food co-op.
6. Plant a garden.
7. Buy in larger quantities.
8. Set a per-serving cost limit and stick to it.
9. Quit eating out.
10. Do not buy frozen foods or pre-packaged meals.
11. Quit eating breakfast.
12. Quit buying "junk foods."

Once these suggestions are offered, the family has a beginning place for evaluating each one. It will be obvious that some do not meet the criteria the family has set up. Others are not serious suggestions. But regardless of their value, the list gives them something to work with.

Step Five: Select the Best Possible Solution or Solutions

This step is a matter of evaluation. Take the criteria that you or your group established in Step Three. Then take each of the possible solutions which came to light during the brainstorming of Step Four. If one of the suggestions clearly cannot meet one of the criteria, then you should discard it or at least set it aside. It may be that you will discover that one or more of the criteria are unrealistic. You may have to revise or discard them. Those decisions will be made during the process of completing Step Five.

Once you have discovered which of the possible solutions meet all the criteria, then you will want to look at them carefully. You will have to weigh their relative merits and make a value judgment about which is best for you or for your group. It may be that the combination of several solutions will be desirable. It might be that several of the solutions can be used in stages.

In this stage of problem solving, it is important for you to remember that your own biases may get in your way. Sometimes you might set up obstacles by your own mental habits which may prevent you from recognizing a good solution even when isolated. To demand that all solutions conform with past experiences is a narrow outlook. It will cause you to overlook a novel idea which might be a good solution.

A group of administrators in one large school district wrestled at length with a plan for the school calendar for the coming year. The date of Easter for the next year came very late in the spring. There was no way to give the customary week's vacation without conflicting with some other long established school activities. Suddenly one member asked why the Easter Vacation had to occur at Easter. "Why," he wondered aloud, "couldn't it come earlier and be called a 'Spring Break'?" There was no reason. Revising the calendar in that manner solved the immediate problem. It also established a new school calendar which the district still uses. This good idea came up only because the group was able to look beyond tradition and see that a novel idea was possible.

Another danger at this stage when you are evaluating possible solutions is the problem of "thinking in a rut." How many of the items which we take for granted are a reality because someone refused to listen to the "rut" thinking around them? The automobile exists in spite of the fact that early inventors were scorned and ridiculed. The airplane is a part of our lives even though the Wright Brothers were told that it could not work.

It is not just in the dramatic inventions that "rut" thinking can hinder. If you automatically reject solutions because "we don't do it that way," then you are allowing what *is* to limit what *could be*. Finally, it has often been observed that it is a good thing the bumblebee can't read, for it would learn that according to engineers, it can't fly.

A negative approach at this stage of problem solving will defeat the process. If the possible solutions meet the criteria you have established, then accept them and move on to determine if they can be implemented. Do not kill them before you have tested them.

As an Individual: Eleven year-old Jennifer has completed her list of possible ways to spend her money. She has to choose the best solution. One criterion that her solution has to meet is the approval of her parents. Another is that she must feel some sense of pleasure as a reward for her hard work. As she studies the long list, she crosses off items that would spend the entire amount at once. She wants more than one thing. She enjoys spending and shopping. She also

crosses off saving the entire amount for the same reasons. She crosses off sharing the cost of something with her brother because she knows they would probably quarrel about ownership. In this fashion she works her way through the list. She finally has the following items.
1. Use $10.00 to open my own savings account at the bank.
2. Buy one good record album for my collection. $10.00
3. Buy the new sweater I saw at the store. $13.00
4. Use $5.00 to order new cards to sell.
5. Use $5.00 for entertainment.

Jennifer has discovered that she is able to gain the approval of her parents, to satisfy her own desire for pleasure, and to invest in order to earn more. The fact that she made a list and selected from it has allowed her to devise solutions which were not a part of the initial problem discussion.

As a Group: A group of trainers for industrial sales personnel in charge of teaching the basic training course for a large appliance company is dissatisfied with class response. They decide that the teaching of the course is at fault, and they want to solve that problem. They call a series of meetings.

They set up the following criteria:
1. The lesson periods must get the material across effectively.
2. The lesson units must fit the 60 minute training periods.
3. The lesson units should be interesting and relevant.

They brainstorm all the possible techniques of teaching they can think of. Their list is long and impressive. Then they compare it to the criteria. They discover that all of the suggested methods of presentation can meet the criteria at times. Lecture, often thought to be boring, can be very interesting if combined with other forms and if given in an enthusiastic manner. As the group works its way through the list, the members realize that the solution is to combine all the techniques. They further realize that variety rather than technique is the answer.

Their next task is to implement that combination in such a way as to achieve the results of better class response.

Step Six: Plan for Implementing the Solution

The final step in problem solving is to decide how the solution which you have selected can be put into effect. This may either be the simplest or the most difficult step in the process.

If the implementation is a matter of your own action and involves simply carrying out some well established procedure, then this step is easy. If, however, you have devised something new and different, or you have set an entire process into motion, it may be that planning for implementation will be crucial and difficult. Implementation is the final test of how effective your problem solving process has been. If your solution cannot be applied, it has little real value.

It may be that if your group has examined a national problem, there will be no way for you to implement the solution by direct personal action. You may need, instead, to plan how groups with jurisdiction in the area could implement the action and then to convey that information to them.

You may also find that putting your solution into effect creates another problem for you. You may need to acquire the skills necessary to implement your solution. You may even find that the solution is so difficult to implement that it makes learning to live with the problem the only real solution. If this is true, the process has not been a waste of your time. It has led you to the point where you can accept the existence of the problem because the alternatives are even worse. To the extent that you accept it, it then ceases to be a problem for you.

As an Individual: Ruth finds that her parents are unable to give her financial assistance for college. She then begins to collect data about scholarships which are available. She writes to the colleges she is most interested in and inquires about financial assistance. She asks particularly about programs for black students. She contacts a local Businesswomen's Club. She talks to her counselor. Once she has all the data, she lists the criteria that any solution has to meet. She decides that she will accept financial assistance unless it requires so much work that it interferes with her classes. She decides any assistance must allow her to major in the area in which she is interested. She will also not accept assistance from groups whose ideas she does not share. The assistance must be enough to meet the cost of her college.

Next, Ruth lists every possible source of financial aid she has found. She then eliminates those that do not meet the criteria she has outlined. Her plan of implementation is simple. She systematically applies for all grants and scholarships which meet the criteria. She applies for government loans which are available. She also joins a student placement service in search of part-time jobs. As the colleges respond, she keeps a tabulation of the total amount of assistance she can get at each of the schools that accept her. As soon as she is sure that she has an adequate amount of money to attend each of the schools, she applies for admission. Eventually, she will have to decide which school to attend. Her successful experience with problem solving in one area will furnish her the means of applying it to a new problem.

As a Group: A summer High School Debate Institute is held on the campus of a large western state university. The staff meets following the conclusion of the institute. They want to examine problems which they have had and design solutions for the next year. One problem which they discuss is that of student research. The staff feels that the students spent too much of their time in their rooms filing debate evidence furnished by the institute, and too little of their time doing original research in the extensive university library.

As the staff works through the problem solving sequence, they determine that the cause of this problem is the pressure on the student to have ample evidence filed and ready to use in the end-of-the-institute debate tournament. Thus, the students choose to file the evidence they are given rather than to seek for more. The staff determines, however, that the tournament has value. They are unwilling to eliminate it.

The staff members decide that the solution must allow students to accumulate and file prepared evidence, and at the same time must allow time for library research. Out of the long list of possibilities, the staff finally decides that the students will be sent the handbook evidence at least three weeks in advance of the institute. They will be instructed to have it filed before reporting to the campus.

The implementation of this solution proves to be complex. Individual staff members are assigned certain areas for research. The deadlines have to be early to allow time for mailing the evidence. One staff member has to prepare detailed filing instructions which must accompany the evidence itself. Finally, the institute schedule has to be revised. It must allow for the additional research time the students will have when freed from the task of filing evidence. As each of these obstacles is anticipated and worked out, the problem nears a solution.

Summary

The six steps in problem solving are a structured reflection of the way our minds work when we think. If we understand this process and continue to apply it, we will be successful in problem solving.

Successful problem solvers usually share three common characteristics. They are usually flexible. Even though they apply the sequence for problem solving, they are able to adapt and to adjust the process when necessary. They are usually realistic. They are willing to compromise, to accept small gains, to recognize what can be. They usually operate with a sense of time. They are aware that sometimes one can work through the process slowly and methodically. At other times, solutions must come quickly and often intuitively.

The problem-solving sequence is one in which you can adapt yourself to the prevailing situation and conditions. It is not rigid. It is not the only method by which people can reach satisfactory courses of action and thought. It is a way, however, which has proved effective for many. We are most often ineffective in problem solving when the problems involve other people. In this case we especially need to be able to apply skills which will allow us to eliminate the mistakes which emotion and conflict sometimes produce.

The next section of this book contains a group of problem situations which you could encounter as an individual or a group. Use them for practice in applying the six steps of problem solving which we have presented.

III. Problems Practiced: Discussion and Role Playing for Problem Solving

You have now been introduced to the need for successful problem solving and to the steps by which problems may be solved. The purpose of this section of the book is to give you some practice in developing the skills of problem solving. Some of these exercises you will need to do alone, often using paper and pen to put the ideas into tangible form. Others will require that you work with another person, or in a group. You and your teacher can choose the appropriate exercise for the goal you have at a given time.

Remember that problem solving depends mainly on two things. First, you must know the steps and apply them. Second, you must avoid the pitfalls which often interfere with problem solving. Both of these can be accomplished by practice. Part III gives you the materials for practice.

Brain Teasers for Warm-up

It is often important to use the mental process in a "stop action" way in order to be able to examine it and understand it. Because our minds work so fast, however, it is difficult to do that. Use the following "brain teaser" in order

38 *Successful Problem Solving*

to keep track of the process your mind goes through in problem solving. You may discover some of the things you are doing wrong.

Directions: Read the following problem description carefully. As you read, have paper and pen handy, and as soon as you begin to look for clues and reach decisions, put down your thoughts as they occur, continuing to record them until you have reached a definite solution to the problem. Then look over the process as you recorded it. Was it in a logical sequence? Did you make use of the system we have studied? Did you have to use one clue or many to solve the problem?

Compare your answer and your process with another classmate. Discuss the differences and similarities.

"The deserted picnic:

A man walking in the country one fine summer evening came upon a tablecloth spread on the ground. Four places were laid, as if for a meal. The food on three of the plates had been almost entirely consumed, while the food on the fourth plate seemed to be untasted. Some of the food was still warm to the touch, and a fire was still burning, though the logs had been scattered. Articles of clothing and other personal belongings had been left, but no signs of disorder were visible. Further observation showed two facts that seemed to deserve attention. The fourth (untouched) plate had very little food upon it, and no knife seemed to have been provided for the person who was to eat from it. A piece of paper large enough to hold half a pound of butter still showed traces of butter, but no butter was anywhere in sight. There were no people to be seen anywhere in the neighborhood."[1]

It is often important to observe and trace group behavior in problem solving in order to understand how groups work together. Use the following "brain teaser" in small groups. Have a group recorder keep track of how often individuals in the group speak, what kinds of contributions they make, and who they talk to. After your group has agreed on a solution, have all groups report to one another. Have each recorder report on what he/she observed about the group process. Discuss the positive and the negative things which were observed.

Directions: Read the following problem description carefully. Work together as a group to decide how to solve the problem.

"Three missionaries (M_1, M_2, M_3) and three Cannibals (C_1, C_2, C_3) are on the A-side of a river. Get them across to the B-side by means of a boat that holds only two people at a time. All the missionaries and one cannibal (C_1) can row.

Never, under any circumstances may the missionaries by outnumbered by the cannibals (except, of course, when there are no missionaries present.)"[2]

Exercises for Understanding Personal Factors in Problem Solving

Role playing can help us understand some of the effects of personal factors which are present in problem solving. Too often when elements such as age or sex are interfering in problem solving, we are unable to get an objective view of the process because we are too emotionally involved. Thus, it is useful to play roles in the classroom that will show these factors and will allow us to view them without emotion.

Directions: Select members of the class to "role play" the following two situations. Allow them a reasonable amount of time to develop a sense of the role they are in. Remind them that they are to respond to one another as realistically as possible.

The large group is to observe and to write down reactions and observations as the role playing is done. Ask them to be aware for times in the role playing when the situation could have been handled differently. Ask them to try to isolate reasons why it was not.

1. (1 female; 2 males)

Situation: The new female foreman in a plant that produces electronic components observes that two men who are very good workers and who have been employed for 10 years by the company are taking increasingly long coffee breaks.

2. (2 females; 1 male)

Situation: A door-to-door salesman of cooking ware is making a scheduled demonstration at a prospective purchaser's house. The housewife's teenage daughter needs her advice about some decisions she has to make immediately.

---

[1] Max Black, *Critical Thinking* (New York: Prentice Hall, Inc., 1952), p. 287.
[2] Patricia Hull Baudendistel, *Teacher's Edition—Person to Person*, Skokie, Ill.: National Textbook Company 1979), p. 193.

Follow-up: As a group, have the class discuss their observations. Particularly consider (1) What effects did age or sex play in these problem situations? (2) Did the individuals give evidence of properly defining and limiting the problem they were faced with? (3) Could they have handled the situation differently with different definitions and limitations of the problems?

Groups, too, are affected by personal factors. Often it is difficult to realize the effects because they are making you think and behave in a particular way. Through the following exercise, you will be able to observe this a little better because you will be role playing. Throughout the exercise be especially aware of your own reactions.

Directions: This is a role playing exercise. It will ask you, in different roles, to examine a situation which is drawn from a modern social experience which often poses problems in many groups.

Divide the class into small groups of 5–7 members. Assign each group one of the group roles listed. Be sure that every group has a different role.

Group Roles:
A police traffic division squad
Student Government Association officers
The School Administration
The Church Board of Elders or Deacons
A real estate firm
The board of directors of the Community Theatre
The Chamber of Commerce
A labor union
A football team

Situation: Bill Morris is an outstanding leader in the group. He is effective in his assigned role, and his is popular and respected. Just this morning, to everyone's great surprise, Bill revealed to your group that he is a homosexual. Now you must discuss what action, if any, your group should take.

Assignment: Each group meets simultaneously. You have 30 minutes to produce your recommendations.

Follow-up: Compare group recommendations. Try to examine two main elements. (1) Are the recommendations of each group affected by the interests and identities of that group? (2) Did any of the groups consider Bill's best interests?

In general discussion, each student should be encouraged to examine personal reactions during the discussion groups. Did age, sex, religion create particular reactions to the problem? Did these factors interfere with objectivity?

Exercises in Defining and Limiting the Problem

Directions: Assume that you are individually faced with each of the following problem situations. Define and limit the scope of each one. Remember that this process should furnish you with a well-worded question which specifies the exact focus your problem solving will follow.

Follow-up: When you have finished, compare your questions with those of at least one other classmate. Discuss the differences between your ideas. Try to determine which ones have the more accurate grasp of the problem.

1. Betty Moore has just been hired to replace the night manager of the local pizza parlor. The person she is replacing was very popular with the employees as well as the customers. When she comes in to observe the operation for a few nights before taking over, she realizes that the man she is replacing can do no wrong in the eyes of the employees.

Her employer, however, tells her in confidence that the efficiency rating of the night crew is very low and that there is some question about the financial reports. He tells her that he wants her to bring the night operation up to the standards of the performance of the day crew.

On her first night of being in charge, she realizes that everyone is watching her very closely. They are comparing her with the person she has replaced.

Define and limit Betty Moore's problem.

2. John is 15. He is the eldest of two boys and a girl in the Atkins family. He makes only average grades in school, but he is very popular among teachers and students. He loves music and is a very talented guitarist, vocalist, and composer. He wants to start a rock group to play at the local teenage disco during the summer.

Mr. Atkins is a stocky former college football player who is a deputy in the county sheriff's office. He rides herd on John continuously over his style of dress, hair, and speech. He is critical of his choice of friends, and, most of all, he objects to the time John devotes to music.

"I never thought I'd see the day when my son would prefer music to sports," he has often commented. The tension is constant and there seems to be no way to ease it.

Define and limit John Atkin's problem.

3. Eric is four. He has been a sunny child with a smooth disposition. He is told that a new baby will soon come to live in the home, and he is very delighted. His talk and his planning all center around the new arrival. When his mother and new sister come home from the hospital, Eric seems very proud of her. He beams when others come to say how pretty she is. He is anxious to help with her.

After about a month, however, Eric begins to change his disposition. He is no longer amiable, jolly and even-tempered. He flies into tantrums. He refuses to go to sleep and is constantly contrary. Punishment by his father seems to make the problem worse.

Define and limit the problem of Eric's parents.

4. Suzanne Johnson is a new member of the school pep club. She feels that the membership is an honor and a big responsibility. She is anxious to begin the work of the organization. On the campus at noon, however, she overhears a conversation between two members who are criticizing the officers and who are planning to quit the group. She realizes that they are spreading this kind of talk among the membership.

Several other girls who are new members of the group then tell Suzanne that the sponsors are unfair and that new members have to do all the work. They indicate that a form of favoritism is shown to those who have been in the club before.

She has already invested $50.00 in her uniform and has signed up for three of the bus trips to out-of-town games.

Define and limit Suzanne Johnson's problem.

5. Jane Allison has worked for over a year to set up the appearance of a senator at the annual Future Farmer's Banquet. She and the other officers of the group have publicized his coming, and many members of the community have said they are coming in honor of the occasion. Three weeks before the banquet, the senator's secretary calls to report, regretfully, that the senator's calendar has become too crowded to allow him the time out of Washington to return home as he had planned. He offers to send one of his legislative assistants.

Define and limit Jane Allison's problem.

Directions: Divide the class into groups of 5-7 members.

Each group is to choose one of the following problem areas and as a group to define and limit a specific problem within that area which a group could approach through the six step sequence we have studied.

Each group is to word the specific problem as a question.

Follow-up: When all groups have finished, read the discussion questions aloud to the entire class. Through class discussion, decide which ones will lead to good group process and why.

Problem Areas:
a. Nuclear energy.
b. Television.
c. Foreign policy.
d. Educational standards.
e. Medical costs.
f. Tax reform.
g. National defense.
h. Drug addiction.
i. Inflation.
j. Gasoline rationing.
k. Unemployment.
l. Divorce.
m. Crime.

Exercises in Analyzing the Problem and Gathering Data

Directions: Analyze each of the situations below by deciding what the probable cause or causes of the problem might be.

1. Betty Collins teaches English Literature at Prescott High School. Betty is conscientious about her subject matter, and has high standards. For the past three days, Betty has been ill. During her absence, Edna Ferguson, the Dramatics Coach, has taken over her classes.

When Betty returns from her absence, she seems to be faced with an outright "revolt" by her students. It seems that Edna has really "turned her classes on." Her students constantly talk about how they like Miss Ferguson. While she had taught them, she had divided the group into teams and generated all types of discussion about problems, philosophies, and ideas of the literary characters they had studied.

The situation has upset Betty a great deal. She was particularly hurt when she overheard one of her favorite students comment to another that Miss Ferguson was a better teacher than she.

2. Mrs. Charlotte Emerson is a white teacher newly employed to teach in an integrated Chicago school. Her classes are made up primarily of black pupils. Charlotte feels that she is a good teacher and she likes order in her class. She also likes for a class to move along at a progressive pace. She was highly successful at her last school in a white suburb of Detroit.

Periodically, the black pupils in one of Charlotte's classes let her know that she is "strict." They imply that the black teachers in the school are "better teachers for them." When Charlotte gives a weekly test, they say, "Other teachers don't give weekly tests."

Charlotte finds that if she counters with power or punishment, she creates a communication distance with the class. She also feels guilty. On the other hand, if she "gives in" and relaxes her standards, the class uses the same tactic the next time she makes an assignment.

3. James King is an old friend of Edward Saxon's from college days. They have kept in touch through the years and still visit occasionally. Ed admires James because he is a hard worker. He has always considered James to be a person of sound judgment. When a vacancy occurs in Ed's office, he asks James to recommend a promising young engineer who would like a career opportunity. James asks Ed to interview his new son-in-law.

Ed talks to the young man, John Biggs. He finds John to be bright, personable, and eager. Furthermore, his references and work record are impressive. Edward decides to hire him.

After about a month, however, Ed begins to wonder if he did the right thing. John often comes late, takes long coffee breaks, and once did not report for work at all. Not only that, his work is not up to the standards Edward expects.

Ed checks the records again. No previous employer had these problems with John. Ed discreetly checks to see if there are problems in the young marriage, but discovers this is not so. Yet, John's poor record of work continues.

Directions: If you were part of a group participating in a problem solving discussion dealing with one of the following areas, where would you go for information? Give specific references you would use.

1. Welfare Reform
2. Improved Work Study Programs

3. Declining Enrollment in Fine Arts Courses
4. Juvenile Delinquency
5. Agricultural Subsidies
6. The Dangers of Excess Credit Buying

The testing of data for reliability is a very important part of the process of gathering information for problem solving. Your ability to test data depends upon careful thought about the standards the data will have to meet in order for you to accept it. Those standards depend many times on the kind of problem being considered.

Directions: Assume that you must collect the data involved in each of the following situations. Make a list of very specific things that would be necessary before you would accept data as valid for that problem. What kinds of information would you need? Where would you look for it?

1. The local United Taxpayers Association has charged that the City Council has not made the best possible use of city funds. They have not brought any charges of graft or theft, but have simply insisted that the council has been wasteful with public monies. The mayor has appointed a committee of citizens to study the situation. You are one of the members of that committee.

2. The members of your fraternity want to set up an amateur radio station in the fraternity house. No one in the fraternity has an amateur ratio license, and the sponsors do not know whether it is permissible to operate such a station even though it would be mainly for transmission within the immediate vicinity of the house. As an officer in the fraternity, you are part of the group who must investigate.

3. A group of students want additional student parking facilities on the campus. They petition the administration to provide it. The administration responds that there is no available land near the campus and that land already owned by the school is set aside for future projects. The students decide to find out if some possible solution has been overlooked. You are one of the students.

4. The new addition to the bank where you are employed is to be named after the original founder. There is to be a dedication ceremony with appropriate speeches. The President of the bank has asked you to provide a 20-minute talk in which you praise the original founder and indicate the reasons his name was chosen for the addition. The man has been dead for forty years, and none of his family live in the area any longer.

46   *Successful Problem Solving*

5. You are a newly commissioned officer in the Air Force. Your company has run across a reference to a "Blister Club" whose insignia is two winger shoes. From the material in which it was mentioned, he judges that it was a World War II club of some kind, which air force men joined. He wants to find out more about the activity. He wants to know what kind of a club it was, who could join, etc. He asks you to find this information for him.

Exercises in Establishing Criteria for Possible Solutions

Directions: Assume that you are the individual with the problem described in each situation below. Read the description carefully, then make a list of the criteria which you believe the individual should use to evaluate any solution.

Keep in mind the goal you believe the person will have in each situation.

1. Mrs. Edith Holmes, a middle-aged black school teacher with twenty-five years teaching experience, is beginning her first semester in DeZavala High School. The school has an 85 percent Mexican-American student body. Mrs. Holmes has been teaching in a private school for the past five years.

Very soon after the semester begins, Mrs. Holmes becomes aware that Quito Rodriquez is a natural leader among the students in her fourth period class. He is also a threat to her authority. He has never openly challenged her, but in many ways has shown her he just tolerates her.

During a class discussion one day, Quito makes remarks in Spanish to which the class responds by laughing uproariously. Since Mrs. Holmes cannot speak Spanish, she quitely requests that the discussion be in English. Quito responds with snickers. The class laughs, also. Mrs. Holmes feels that in order to retain control of the class, she must win Quito. She quietly asks, "Quito, would you please wait for a minute after class? I want to talk to you."

He looks at her, checks to be sure he has everyone's attention, and answers her with a phrase in Spanish. Some of the boys clap and whistle. Mrs. Holmes ignores the remark and the bell rings. Quito remains in his seat, waiting for Mrs. Holmes to begin talking.

2. Stephen Samuels is 16. His parents have offered him a choice of what he will do for the summer. He has three opportunities which have become open to him. He may take a summer job in an office downtown. The pay is not particularly great, but he will get a chance to do research for a law firm and learn about that

profession. The firm usually offers the job to a student with the understanding that it will be available for all three years of high school. Stephen is sure that if he doesn't take the job another student will take it and keep it for three years.

Stephen also has a trip to Europe to consider. His great aunt, who is very close to him, wants to take him with her to tour Western Europe for six weeks. Stephen's language in school is German. His main interest has been World History and especially the history of the second World War.

Stephen's band director has indicated to him that he has a real chance to become drum major for the band the following year, if he will attend a Band Institute during the summer. The Institute is scheduled during the first three weeks of the summer. Since Stephen intends to major in instrumental music in college, he realizes that the position of drum major is an important one.

It is time to begin applying for admission, getting passport, or accepting the job—depending on which choice Stephen makes. Because of the difficulty of the decision, he has not been able to make up his mind.

3. (This is a true situation) Jed Smock is an evangelist. He travels to college campuses in the South and preaches in the open, in high traffic areas. He comes without advance notice and stays several days.

He preaches without a microphone, for his voice is like a bullhorn. He preaches for hours at a time, and he can be heard inside the buildings near the concourse when he preaches at Auburn University. Some professors find it hard to keep the attention of students while Rev. Smock is preaching outside.

Jed is a hellfire-and-brimstone preacher. However, he has a college education, and he loves to match wits with hecklers. He is a pretty good debater. He always attracts a crowd. Then he preaches—and preaches—and preaches.

He is controversial because he is not bashful about telling his listeners about their sins. Sometimes he charges the professors with wickedness because they place learning above faith. He has said that professors at Auburn "rape the minds" of students, and that all of them should be fired.

Because he attracts a large crowd, the area around him is jammed. Students with no interest in him find it hard to get to class on time. Others who are his followers skip classes to help him and urge others to skip, too. When he leaves, these students often return to class and use the discussion periods to try to evangelize their teachers and other students.

Some of the students and some of the professors have made a formal complaint to the Dean of Student Affairs about Rev. Smock. They ask that he be removed from the campus. They also ask that he be required to get a permit to speak. They charge that he interferes with the learning and teaching process of the university. The Dean must now solve the problem.

Directions: Divide the class into groups of 5-7 members. Choose one of the discussion questions below. Underneath each question, some analysis and data is given which will help you understand the goals of the group.

As a group, make a list of the criteria which you believe should be used in that situation to evaluate solutions.

1. What should be done to strengthen the mathematics program at Central High School?

The latest statistics have just been given to the school board by the Instructional Services Division of the school district. They show that for the fourth year in a row, the SAT and ACT scores have declined at one high school in the area of math. During that same period, the scores in English have stayed the same or increased. This seems to rule out the causes of declining I.Q., deficiencies in the lower grades, and differences in socioeconomic levels. During this same period of time the SAT and ACT scores in both math and English have stayed the same or increased at the other high school in the district. Clearly, there seems to be an indication that something is lacking in the mathematics program itself at Central High School.

2. What can be done to decrease disturbances and drug use at the Community Center during rock concerts?

Two years ago, the city voted a bond issue to build a very modern and spacious community center. The main idea was to provide a place locally where concerts, speakers, and other programs could be held. Among the main reasons citizens gave for voting in favor of the bond was that they wanted more constructive activities for the youth of the city.

An elaborate series of rock concerts has been scheduled in with many big name stars appearing. The concerts are extremely well attended by local young people and many from out of town. The young people are pleased to have such first class entertainment available to them. The city council is pleased because the profit has been significant and the bond indebtedness is being retired more quickly than anticipated.

The problem is that there is an increasing incidence of marijuana and other drugs being used during the concerts. As a result, a number of arrests have taken place and some violence has erupted when law officers have had to take action. This has resulted in some parents demanding that the city council schedule no more rock concerts in the center. It has also brought demands from the students and city young adults that the police stop harrasing people at concerts.

Exercises in Suggesting All Possible Solutions

Directions: You have twenty minutes to brainstorm as many ways as you can think of to use a screwdriver. If you are able to think of more than 20 ways, list them all, but try for at least 20. Remember the rules of brainstorming. *The first 20 minutes is an individual process.*

Follow-up: 1. Have a recorder make a list on the blackboard. Have each student call out his, record them on the board but do not duplicate. It should be interesting to see how many separate things your class found that a simple screwdriver could do. 2. Discuss the brainstorming process. Did you have difficulty thinking of 20 new ways to use a common object? Do you have difficulty breaking out of a "rut" in thinking about solutions? Were there uses on your classmates' lists which you did not think of at all? Did compiling a master list cause you or others to think of additional ideas? What do these suggest about the value of groups in problem solving?

Directions: Divide the class into groups of 5-7. Have all the groups brainstorm for 20 minutes on the following topic: "What can a coathanger be used for?"

Follow-up: Tabulate how many different uses each group got. Then ask each group to decide what things contributed to or hindered their group. Be sure that each group considers all the factors that can affect groups in problem solving.

Exercises in Applying the Six Steps in Problem Solving

Directions: Divide the class into groups of 5-7. Each group is to choose one of the following discussion questions, or formulate one of its own. The group is to follow the six steps in problem solving. The teacher will indicate time and a dead-line for the presentation of the follow-up reports. Several days may be required in order to do a thorough job with the process.

Topics:

1. How can television better serve the needs and interests of the American public?
2. How can a college education be made available to all?
3. How can higher quality teachers be insured for the public schools?
4. How can student government be made more meaningful?
5. How can America solve the energy crisis?
6. How can inflation be halted?

Follow-up: Each group is to present a report to the class which will consist of:
   a. Statement of analysis
   b. Criteria established by the group for solutions
   c. Final solution
   d. Method of implementation
   e. Observations by group about their function as problem solvers

Directions: Assume that you are one of the following individuals:
   a. Superintendent of Schools
   b. Chairman of the English Department
   c. Speech Teacher
   d. President of the Teachers' Union
   e. President of the Student Minority Coalition

Read carefully the problem description below. Then work through the six steps in problem solving, recording your final decisions at each step. You will need to gather data about schools in your own locality, or you can invent data if none is available. (If you do this, be sure to indicate that you have used fictional data.)

Follow-up: Report to the class orally or to your instructor in written form. Indicate the result of each step and carefully explain your solution or solutions to the problem from the point of view of the person whose identity you have assumed.

Situation: At the May 10 meeting of the School Board, Dr. Eunice Morgan, spokesperson for the black community, addressed the board. She voiced concern about the gap between minority and majority children's achievement scores. Dr. Morgan asked the board to listen carefully to the grievances of black teachers, and to bring in black consultants to assist with special learning problems of minority students. Both the superintendent and the board acknowledged that achievement scores for the minority students were unsatisfactory. The superintendent said that part of the school district's five-year plan focuses on teaching methodology, consultants, and staff re-organization which will address the majority-minority achievement gap. Dr. Morgan especially asked that the ratio of minority teachers and administrators be examined to be sure that there was no hiring discrimination. She further charged the superintendent and board with finding the causes of lower achievement by minority students.

Additional Practice Opportunities

A. As an individual or as a class group, use any of the problem situations that were given in the text of Part II in illustration of each new step. Extend the situation into the next step or steps and apply the problem solving sequence.

B. Clip articles from the newspaper that describe problem situations. Attempt to apply the problem solving sequence and record each step as you work through it. Then watch for follow-up articles that indicate how the problem was solved in the real situation. The following are recommended activities to further reinforce your skills in problem solving:

1. Identify presidential decision areas regarding major national problems. Find news and magazine articles that will help you identify cause, effects, and possible solutions. Then, either in written or oral form, attempt to find a workable solution to that particular problem.

2. Seek to identify international problem areas that would best be solved by action from multilateral organizations such as: the UN, Nato, and SEATO. Apply again research techniques that will assist you in finding the best possible solution.

3. Arrange for interviews with the mayor, members of city council, the superintendent of schools, members of the school board, or other members of the community who are in decision-making positions. Take a real problem that they are facing and follow through the problem solving sequence.

C. Be aware of problem situations that develop in your own school, home, or place of employment. If you are not immediately involved, attempt to apply the problem solving steps anyway. Watch to see how the people involved do solve the problem. If you are actually involved in the situation, make a conscientious effort to apply the steps of problem solving and to make those around you aware of how you are working to solve the situation.

D. Take a problem faced by a character in literature or one faced by a person in history. Ignore what was done in the fictional or real-life situation. Isolate information needed for successful problem solving and apply yourself to finding the best solution. Discover the difference in thought process. Examples in fiction that you can use are: Hamlet, Macbeth, Holden Caulfield from *Catcher in the Rye,* Huck Finn, or Ralph from *Lord of the Flies.* Examples that can be used from history are: Franklin D. Roosevelt, Abraham Lincoln, or Richard Nixon.